50 Great Ideas

LinkedIn for Business

Boring but important stuff

This book is not intended to provide personalised legal, financial or investment advice. The authors and the publisher specifically disclaim any liability, loss or risk, which is incurred as a consequence, directly or indirectly, of the use and application of any contents of this work. So use some common sense!

Cover design: Tom O'Ryan, JC Social Media

Copyright © 2019 JayBee Media Limited

The right of Jodie and Ben Cook to be identified as the author of this work has been asserted in accordance with the Copyright Designs and Patents Act 1988.

All rights reserved. No part of this work may be reproduced in any material form (including photocopying or storing in any medium by electronic means and whether or not transiently or incidentally to some other use of this publication) without the written permission of the copyright holder except in accordance with the provisions of the Copyright, Designs and Patents Act 1988. Applications for the copyright holder's written permission to reproduce any part of this publication should be addressed to the publishers.

This book is not affiliated with LinkedIn.

About the authors

Experienced in all aspects of digital marketing, Jodie started JC Social Media, a social media agency that represents and advises clients all over the world, in 2011. The company has worked with a wide range of businesses from independents to global brands, and helped to market hundreds of businesses online.

Jodie regularly contributes comments to news outlets including the BBC, ITV and Forbes, on social media topics. She has been listed in The Drum's "30 women in tech under 30", Management Today's "35 women in business under 35" and Computer Weekly's "rising stars" in tech.

Ben is a full spectrum digital marketing expert with specific knowledge in search engine marketing, conversion rate optimisation and, of course, social media. The combination of these skills helps companies increase and convert overall web traffic, with a significant and measurable impact on the bottom line.

The 50 Great Ideas series was created after the two began brainstorming the ideas that really make a difference to a company's digital presence. Their aim is to provide simple and effective, actionable tactics for the beginner, intermediate and advanced digital marketer to generate better return from social media.

Introduction

Welcome to **50 Great Ideas for LinkedIn**. Pardon the clichés but, yes, it does what it says on the tin and, in this case, you'd do well to judge a book by its cover. Herein lies 50 unique, effective and great ideas for LinkedIn.

LinkedIn is one of our favourite social media platforms for the following reasons:

- You know exactly who someone is and what they do.
- Your message to someone is likely to land in their hands rather than be filtered by a secretary or other gatekeeper.
- It's akin to a business card book, except it updates itself!

LinkedIn is all about finding an excuse to get in contact with someone.

LinkedIn, used well, takes the concept that *it's not what you know, but who*, much further. Upon reading and acting on these ideas you will realise that *who you know* is more powerful than you had ever imagined.

In this book you'll find a range of ideas to help you market yourself or your business through LinkedIn. From profile-optimisation to advanced searches; from tips and tricks to filter out any time-wasters to making sure you stick to the features of LinkedIn that will grow your business.

Note:

In some ideas we have included links to where you can do this on LinkedIn.

All information about the platform and its users is correct at the time of writing and publication but, as you'll appreciate, things move quickly in the world of social media and whilst we'll endeavour to keep things updated, please tell us if something has changed! That would really help. In fact, if you have any comments and thoughts on the book, we'd love to hear them.

Feel free to tweet Jodie @cookiewhirls any time and do check out the other titles in the series.

Happy social networking!

Explaining the ratings

Each idea is rated on the ease of its implementation and how effective it is overall. We also indicate how often you should carry out each tactic.

We recommend that you implement some of the tactics immediately since they're essentially profile optimisations. The ideas that can be implemented on a daily basis tend to form part of your everyday content creation and distribution or effective lead-generation techniques.

The 'effect' rating (from one to five stars) represents the kind of impact that a specific tactic has for any given business. We haven't included any less than 2 stars. Anything with four and five stars means they form a core element of your LinkedIn activity and/or should result in improved reach, engagement and lead-generation over time.

The 'ease' rating represents how quickly and simply the tactic can be delivered. The higher the rating, the easier and simpler the tactic is to complete. A five star rating means the idea is easy to implement or that the change will make an immediate impact, or both! A one star might represent something that takes a long time to take effect or that perhaps requires in depth knowledge or skill. Yes, there is a one star rated tactic!

What this means is that the quick wins, those tactics with a pair of four or five star ratings, should be done by everyone and now! These should be right at the top of your priority list. You can then work on the ones that either require a little more time and expertise or have less of an impact.

We've put together a handy checklist in printable format available from www.jcsocialmedia.com/great-ideas

Idea 1: Use a professional headshot

Having a professional headshot on your personal LinkedIn profile is so important. Making eye contact and a friendly smile at the people who may be your next clients or suppliers works wonders for your personal brand.

Hopefully many of you already have one, but it is amazing how many people who rely on LinkedIn for lead-generation and brand awareness have low quality, unprofessional or seriously dated LinkedIn pictures. Your profile underpins the success of many of the ideas and tactics we'll explore.

Even if you think you have a great headshot, ask yourself the following questions:

- Do I look approachable and trustworthy?
- Do I look like an expert in my field?
- Am I recognisable?
- Will this person deliver?

If all of your answers are 'yes' – ask some of your (ruthlessly) honest friends the same questions.

Top tips for making sure your headshot cuts the mustard:

- Ensure it was taken within the last two years
- Make sure your hair style and hair colour are the same as you have now
- If possible, get one professionally taken (it is worth it!)
- Be in a studio or the environment in which you

work
- Use a plain background
- Be on your own

The worst pictures we've found include those taken in a nightclub and selfies!

How often: ASAP, and then every couple of years
Ease/time: 3
Effect: 5

Idea 2: Ensure you're connected to everyone in your existing network

I've never met anyone who hasn't been able to add at least ten people when I've asked them to really think hard of possible contacts. Your network of first-degree connections is really important on LinkedIn, as we will discover throughout this book. Most people, however, are missing out some obvious connections that they should be LinkedIn with.

Family members, close school and university friends, work colleagues – it's not just about business and industry contacts; all of these individuals could have links to the people you need to speak to.

People you may know:

- Those you went to school, college or university with
- Suppliers of your company
- Clients of your company
- Colleagues from a previous role
- Family members
- Friends
- People within your current company
- People met at networking events
- Those belonging to the same organisations or societies as you
- People you know from the gym, pub, or other social activities

Ask these people to connect and add a personal message. It will make the rest of the tips much more fruitful! Remember to only add people that you actually know (more in idea 4).

Pro tip: go to 'my network > add connections' or select the option to import connections from a file or search your address book.

How often: ASAP then as required
Ease/time: 4
Effect: 3.5

Idea 3: Use the LinkedIn app to search your phone contacts

This is a neat trick to help with idea 2. You can use the LinkedIn mobile app to search your phone contacts for people you're not connected with on LinkedIn. If no new connections are found, that's reassurance that you're effectively adding to your network as you go.

Download the LinkedIn app from the app store then, when prompted, let it access your contacts and add those with whom you're not yet connected.

How often: ASAP
Ease/time: 4.5
Effect: 3.5

Idea 4: Don't just link in with everyone and anyone

Yes, you want to link in with all of your personal network but don't get all trigger-happy on the 'connect' button. The more connections you have, the better, but adding people you don't genuinely know dilutes the strength of your network. They're less likely to engage with your posts and they won't be able to introduce you to 2nd degree contacts if they happen to be one of your mutual connections.

Sharing a handful of connections or being at the same networking event does not warrant a connection unless someone sends a decent message to explain the situation, as per idea 17.

Pro tip: when deciding whether or not to ask someone, answer this question: would I feel comfortable asking this person for an introduction to someone they know?

How often: Avoid it – be picky.
Ease/time: 4
Effect: 2

Idea 5: Write your summary from the heart

Some would describe one's LinkedIn profile as their "online CV". If that's the case, then your summary is your covering letter.

The summary is not just another area to plug with keywords and phrases about your business; you can do this in the 'experience' section. Here's where you portray your ideas, passions and personality.

Include things like:

- Why you're in your career or why you started your business
- The passion that drives you and where it came from
- The best part of your work
- Who you enjoy working with
- Who is it you want to help
- Your interests outside work

Write it in first person (no exceptions) and have one person in mind when you are writing it – perhaps your best client.

Just like when writing your CV and covering letter: proof, proof and proof.

Pro tip: finally, explain how is best to contact you.

How often: ASAP, update as needed.
Ease/time: 2.5
Effect: 4

Idea 6: Take control of your public profile

LinkedIn lets you decide the information available to LinkedIn members with whom you are not connected. This is known as your 'public profile'.

At the time of writing, this link takes you there:

https://www.linkedin.com/psettings/

When you are logged in and on this page, you will see there is a list of aspect of your LinkedIn profile you can edit.

Go through these points to change the appearance of your profile to someone who is or isn't connected to you. The left hand side shows what your profile will look like to this person.

It is completely up to you, but we recommend:

Going to 'Edit public profile' and ensuring 'Your profile's public visibility' is set to 'on'.

Then ticking the following boxes:

- ✔ Profile photo - public: so people know they have found the right person
- ✔ Headline: it's a nice 120-character summary of what you do
- Summary: which should be a first-person account of why you do what you do

- Current experience: So people see where you work and how long you've been there.
- Honours and awards: this adds credibility

We recommend un-ticking the following profile sections to people who aren't connected to you. This is the information people will see once you have accepted them as a connection, but only then.

- Details of current experience
- Past experience
- Education
- Any personal information

Your contact details will be shared when you connect with people. Make sure these aren't contained within your summary, but you may wish to indicate your preferred contact method there, as per the pro tip in idea 5.

Any profile sections that LinkedIn includes but we haven't listed here are down to personal preference, we'll let you decide!

How often: Once
Ease/time: 3
Effect: 3

Idea 7: Change your profile URL.

The default URL for your profile takes the format linkedin.com/in/your-name-4f-2s-7h.

It's a lesser-known feature of LinkedIn but it means that you will have a neat and tidy URL.

You can change your profile URL by using the same link as in the previous tip:

https://www.linkedin.com/psettings/

Under the heading 'your public profile URL' in the top right hand corner, click the pen icon to change the URL if you haven't already.

The easiest thing to use is your full name, but if someone already has it, LinkedIn will suggest other variations. You could, alternatively, use your Twitter or Instagram username for consistency.

How often: Once
Ease/time: 4
Effect: 2

Idea 8: Add files to your summary

This simple step makes your profile look seriously impressive and provides backing for everything you've mentioned in the summary. Any news stories or publications you've been in should be presented here.

What you can upload:

- YouTube, Vimeo video links
- PDFs (menus, press features, brochures)
- Images (team pictures, images that illustrate your services, images of products)
- Anything else on the 'supported providers' list

Pro tip: this feature of LinkedIn uses embed.ly, so you can see the full and ever-increasing list of what you can upload here:

http://embed.ly/providers

How often: ASAP and on-going
Ease/time: 3.5
Effect: 5

Idea 9: Choose 6-8 skills to be endorsed for

You might be an expert in hundreds of different skills but you're much better off looking like an expert in a small number than being a jack of all trades. By concentrating on just a handful of skills, you can rapidly grow endorsements in those areas.

There are some skills that are very closely related and some that don't really mean anything. Take 'strategy' and 'business strategy', for example. Unless you're a 'strategy consultant' and strategy really is your thing, you'd be far better off collecting all those endorsements under 'business strategy' – it means more.

Click 'profile > edit profile'. Go down the list of skills on your profile and click 'x' on any that aren't relevant to your work, until the best 6-8 are left. The sooner you do this, the sooner you start accumulating endorsement in the right fields.

How often: Choose them now, carefully consider any future changes
Ease/time: 5
Effect: 4

Idea 10: Complete your profile

Well, duh?!

But don't tell us this idea is a cop out because we could have easily strung this out into ten different points. The fact is you need to have past positions, your education, skills, publications and other details completed.

Some people use LinkedIn extensively and, therefore, set a lot of stall by the quality, depth and attention to detail of your profile. Filling in as much as you can, as best as you can, really helps paint the picture of a professional.

By listing your schools, university, volunteering roles, awards, etc., you have more areas in common with your connections. This helps build a rapport before you've even met someone.

This process should be time-consuming; you should be thinking carefully about each and every section of your profile, ensuring it reads well and is error-free. You may need to revisit elements of your profile as your career and achievements develop or as you remember more details.

Pro-tip: when describing past positions in your 'experience' section; tailor them to the skills and interests you have in your current role. Even completely random job roles will have some crossover of skill or interest so ensure they're listed.

(We have a series of 10 LinkedIn profile optimisation emails that you can sign up to here: http://eepurl.com/boCUp5).

How often: ASAP
Ease/time: 2
Effect: 5

Idea 11: Contact information

Ensure your contact details are up to date and accurate, especially if you've moved role recently and if you no longer use a certain email address; you don't want important emails building up in an inbox you don't check!

1. Ensure your email address is your work email address. LinkedIn is clever and will show you people you have previously emailed as potential connections, and will do the same to them.

2. Add your work address (not a home address) as this helps you to be found in location searches.

3. Add up to three websites. You don't have to use LinkedIn's pre-written website titles when naming them. Instead use 'other' and then rename with your own choice of title.

4. Add your Twitter account if you keep it updated

How often: Just once and then every time your details change
Ease/time: 4.5
Effect: 4

Idea 12: Engage with your network

The more active you are on LinkedIn, the more people will see your name and maybe navigate to your profile. Simples. Liking people's updates, sharing them (if appropriate) and leaving comments will elevate your profile quickly. And since your profile is now so amazing, this is ideal.

This is both a perfect way to stay in the minds of your connections but get your name in front of other members within theirs.

Pro-tip: don't overdo it! If you like and share everything you see, people will think of you as a spammer (or that you have waaay too much time on your hands. Try to leave a few thoughtful and extended comments per week as opposed to ten "well done" or "nice!" comments every day.

How often: Daily
Ease/time: 4
Effect: 4

Idea 13: View other profiles either in private or public

In your LinkedIn settings you can choose (a) whether other LinkedIn members can see when you've viewed their profile or (b) if you wish to remain anonymous.

Keep the information available (option a) if you want that person to know you've been checking them out. This can be utilised as a bit of an ego stroke, a way of getting on someone's radar or you might be waiting on them for something – it's a very gentle chaser.

Before meeting someone, check out his or her profile. They will see you have done your research. Are you about to cold-call someone? View their profile so they recognise your name, even if subconsciously. Profile hopping can also play a role in your general activity, as per idea 12, above; many will return the favour and check your profile out.

Spend all your time checking out competitors, arch nemeses or secret crushes? That's when to use it privately.

Pro tip: remember it works both ways with LinkedIn. If you don't let people see when you've viewed their profile, you won't know who has viewed yours. This 'who has viewed my profile' feature is very useful, as we'll find out later.

How often: Ongoing
Ease/time: N/A
Effect: 5

Idea 14: View your stats

Now you're more active on LinkedIn, it's a good time to view your personal LinkedIn stats. As we've explained, the more active someone is on LinkedIn, the more profile views they get. You will see evidence of this on your stats graph. The peaks will coincide with various actions; troughs with periods of inactivity.

This is accessed by clicking 'who's viewed your profile' from the LinkedIn homepage. There is far more data available if you have a Premium account, including stats about articles and updates.

With a free account, you're limited to seeing basic data on your articles by clicking 'views of your article' from the left hand side of the home page. You can also access top level information about posts you've shared by selecting 'posts and activity' from the 'me' dropdown.

How often: Weekly
Ease/time: 4
Effect: 4

Idea 15: Use LinkedIn advanced search to find prospects

Have a target company in mind? Maybe you know the exact job title of your best clients. LinkedIn is the perfect place to find them.

Open an advanced search (by clicking 'advanced' next to the search bar at the top of LinkedIn's website) and use the fields to describe your targets. For example, if you sell billboard space in the UK and you usually deal with CMOs, directors of marketing or marketing directors, search for these titles in the UK under the 'keyword' field. If you provide widgets to customers within three specific industries, tick those industries when prompted.

You should be able to find numerous potential leads. These are people you can email, call or send material to. Having a name and knowing which office they work from is vitally important.

Pro tip: narrow down this search by geographic area AND select '2nd connections'. Provided you actually know all of your 1st degree connections personally, asking for an introduction from one of them will be easy.

How often: Monthly
Ease/time: 3
Effect: 4.5

Idea 16: Lead-generation

Once you have found people using your LinkedIn search, or if you already know their names and positions, reach out to people by connecting with them and adding a message.

This approach doesn't have to be salesy, and if someone is in a role where they're likely to be inundated with unsolicited approaches, a sales pitch will simply not work.

Here you have three options, listed below:

1. Send an InMail. This requires a premium LinkedIn account.

2. Send a connection request with a personalised message (explored in idea 17). Some people simply do not accept invitations without a personalised message (particularly because most people haven't yet read idea 19!).

3. Send a connection request without a message. This is impersonal, but may get that initial foot in the door.

Pro tip: a secret extra option involves messaging people who are in the same LinkedIn group as you! To do this, make sure you leave 'group members' ticked when on the advanced search page.

How often: Weekly
Ease/time: 2.5
Effect: 4

Idea 17: Send a personal introduction when connecting

In most cases, you should add a personal message when attempting to connect. Use LinkedIn on a desktop to do this. The mobile app is somewhat of a 'toilet app' (like tinder) and designed to expand your network quickly, with minimal effort or thought.

The personal message could include:

- Why you want to connect
- A mention of any mutual connections you have
- What's in it for them
- Where you have met them before, if you have

You should follow this protocol even if you know the person in question, or if there's a chance they won't recognise you or forget how they know you.

A useful feature of LinkedIn is that each connection's profile you view has a 'relationship' section. This tells you the date you connected and shows any message history you have with them. Being clear in your connection request how you met someone will help to remind you how you know or met this person years later!

How often: When you'd like to connect with someone
Ease/time: 3
Effect: 4

Idea 18: Get LinkedIn premium

If LinkedIn lead-generation is your game, you HAVE to get a premium account. It's about £600 per year depending on which package you go for but it will give you so much more potential when it comes to reaching out to new people. You can send InMail messages to people with whom you're not connected and you'll have a shiny professional profile. Depending on your game, the latter might make it worth it by itself.

Want to try before you buy? Use LinkedIn premium's free month (add your card details and remember to cancel it if you don't want to pay after the month is up) to see what you can achieve with the added features. It's not a magic tool in itself; think of it as supplementing the great work you're already doing in LinkedIn lead-generation.

Pro tip: use the job-hunter profile for many of the benefits of LinkedIn's main premium profile at a lower cost.

How often: Try it as soon as you're confident in your lead-generation activity
Ease/time: 4
Effect: 5

Idea 19: "Reply but don't accept yet"

Keep getting random connection requests and not sure what to do with them? Accepting ones from strangers isn't the best idea, but neither is deleting them.

If someone has found your LinkedIn profile and decided to click to request a connection, there's a reason. The trouble is, if they've not written a message with their request (usually advised!) you have absolutely no idea what that motive is and what's in it for you. But guess what? Some of these people will have a genuine reason for connecting; they might even want your services. Remember that sometimes LinkedIn doesn't even ask you to leave a message; depending in which section of LinkedIn you've clicked 'connect,' it just sends the request immediately, no questions asked.

Use the "reply but do not accept" option to start a conversation. Here's what I use:

"Hi, thanks for your connection request.

Happy to connect, but can I ask how you found my profile or what I can be of assistance with? Sorry if we've met before and I've not recognised you from your picture.

Best wishes, Jodie"

Here's exactly how to get there:

Go to your pending invitations page. Hover over the speech bubble icon. Click the reply arrow. Write your message. If people respond, go you! You've just started a conversation with a potential client. If they don't, no problem! They were probably just looking to add randomers in order to access their connections.

How often: When required
Ease/time: 3
Effect: 4

Idea 20: Tag your important connections

If you have been using LinkedIn for a while you will probably have a lot of connections. A lesser-known feature of LinkedIn is the ability to sort your connections by tagging them. This is now only available with Sale Navigator – one of LinkedIn's Premium offerings.

Tag your connections appropriately in order to keep a closer eye on them. Knowledge is power. To tag a connection, navigate to "my network>connections" and scroll down to the list of your existing connections. You can sort them by name or how recently you added them. Find the connection you're looking for and click the little tag symbol that appears when you hover over them. Create a new tag if required and use this.

You can now filter your contacts by these tags, making it easy to check out what they've each been up to recently.

Pro tip: LinkedIn has it's own CRM follow-up system – you can set reminders on people's profiles for when you want to follow up with them or arrange a meeting. Go to a connection's profile and click the "reminder" button in the "relationship" section.

How often: When you add an important connection
Ease/time: 3
Effect: 3.5

Idea 21: View a specific person's recent activity

With Facebook, it is easy to see what someone has been up to. You simply go to their Facebook profile and scroll down their timeline. With LinkedIn it's not so easy because this isn't how the platform's profiles work.

You can see what someone has shared, liked and commented on recently by typing their name into the top search bar or clicking on their name on your home feed. Next, click the arrow next to the blue 'send a message' button, and select 'view recent activity'.

Use this before you meet a prospect to find out what has interested them recently, or to make sure you have engaged with their updates. It's a perfect place to find conversation starters.

How often: Before you get in touch with someone
Ease/time: 4
Effect: 4

Idea 22: Give genuine recommendations

Recommendations separate the men and women from the boys and girls, and they speak volumes about the work you do. Whilst you can make your profile look great and it's pretty easy to accumulate endorsements, recommendations are somewhat harder to come by.

Of course, *giving* a recommendation isn't difficult – you don't have to ask to give someone one and they'll really appreciate you doing it. Writing recommendations gives you some exposure by being seen on other people's pages and you're much more likely to receive them; both in return from that person if the relationship is collaborative or from someone else you've worked with.

Be genuine when giving a recommendation and be specific about what this person did for you, why you recommend them and the type of business you recommend them to. Remember, the more specific you are about how you worked together, the better idea a third party will have about what you and your business do.

Pro tip: finding a well-connected person who has only a few recommendations will maximise your own exposure from giving a recommendation.

How often: Find some to give now, then a couple per month
Ease/time: 2
Effect: 3

Idea 23: Ask for recommendations

Recommendations separate the men and women from the boys and girls, and they speak volumes about the work you do. Whilst you can make your profile look great and it's pretty easy to accumulate endorsements, recommendations are somewhat harder to come by.

Seen that paragraph somewhere before? Good, you've been paying attention!

We're going to level with you. Unsolicited recommendations do happen, especially if people start reading this book(!), but the majority of them are more forcefully acquired. Most of the time, you'll need to point someone in the right direction and you'll really have to nag some people to do one.

People love reviews and recommendations and a third party's view is very important to them. That's why rating platforms like TripAdvisor have become so influential and why Google and Facebook now have them. They're your way of showing people you're good at what you do.

Start with the easy wins; those people who would love to recommend you publicly. Next, find people who probably would, but don't have the time. Send them a link to your profile, instructions and a couple of lines they could use in the recommendation. Most people will just do it if you've gone to the effort of making it easy for them. Lastly, offer swaps with your collaborators. This strengthens your relationship, gives you another reason to stay in touch and earns you both a recommendation (just make sure you have a few other recommendations on the board before doing this or it's too easy to see you've employed this tactic).

How often: As many as possible now – you can't have too many!
Ease/time: 1.5
Effect: 5

Idea 24: Interact with your collaborators

By 'collaborators' we mean individuals at other companies with whom you share a target audience.

Collaborators and synergistic LinkedIn accounts can provide access to larger audiences and important new contacts. If used correctly, they can be pivotal to your success from a content and profile reach perspective as well as lead-generation.

When interacting with your connections by scrolling your news feed, pay closer attention to those with whom you share an audience. By commenting on and liking their posts, you are then seen by their connections and stay fresh in their mind.

This is made all the easier if you have tagged them as per idea 20.

How often: Weekly
Ease/time: 3
Effect: 3

Idea 25: See the breakdown of your 'followers'

Whilst logged in, click 'Me' from the top menu and then 'Posts & Activity' from the drop down. 'Followers' is found on the left hand side - click on it to see a breakdown of all your followers.

This gives you insight into the make up of your connections plus any additional followers you have by seniority, sector and location. This is particularly useful if you have lots of followers who aren't your connections (if you're a big cheese, basically) but it's interesting and can help shape your efforts and updates.

How often: Every three months, for interest and guidance
Ease/time: 5
Effect: 2

Idea 26: Add value

Whether you're making an update on your personal or business profile, always consider your audience. The best kind of content adds value to your connections and followers, so think carefully about your posts. The more likes, comments and, best of all, shares you generate, the greater the reach of the post and your brand.

The most sharable content resonates with lots of people who, in turn, feel like their connections will benefit from it. This is why infographics and videos do so well.

Depending on your personal or business brand, as well as your sector, adding value is done by entertaining, informing, inspiring and providing insights. Essentially, provoking a positive reaction in someone such that they are compelled to take action in some way.

Examples of how you can add value:

- Share an article you like and explain why you like it in a sentence before linking to it

- Post an image of a product you own or a service you have employed which helps with a certain aspect of your role

- Share news of free downloads you offer on your site or courses you have coming up

- Your own take on a recent change in your industry and what it means for other industries (for example the chancellor's latest budget)

- Videos and infographics you or your team has produced

Pro tip: check that images and videos have formatted properly once you've posted them.

How often: Up to daily
Ease/time: 3
Effect: 3

Idea 27: Share industry facts and figures

A great idea for content is to share industry-specific facts and figures. For most professionals and business people, the ability to portray yourself as an expert is one of the main benefits of the platform.

As per the last idea; the more interesting the better. Interesting and unusual information gives your brand some personality and increases the sharablilty of your content.

This is a tactic utilised across all social networks but with real importance over LinkedIn. Ensure the information you share is up to date and from a reliable source, LinkedIn is probably the only platform where bad information will actually be highlighted.

Examples include:

- 80% of accounts payable professionals believe there is insufficient training provided.

- In 2014, construction contributed 6.5% of the UK's economic output and provided 2.1 million jobs.

- Employees stay at companies on average 50% longer if they receive regular praise for their work.

How often: Weekly

Ease/time: 2.5
Effect: 3

Idea 28: Make your content clear

Potentially, a fair proportion of your LinkedIn updates will attempt to encourage your users to click on a link; whether this is to a blog, an event page or a booking or squeeze page. This goes for updates on both your personal or business pages.

The key is to keep the copy as succinct and effective as possible. Every unnecessary word before the link provides an opportunity for the reader to switch off and keep scrolling. If you're telling a story or pulling out a key insight of the link included, make sure it doesn't waffle.

Signpost clearly what the linked content is about, what problem it solves or who it's appropriate for. Remember, this should be adding value to your audience – make sure they know the post is for their benefit- not yours!

How often: When posting content links
Ease/time: 4
Effect: 4

Idea 29: Share original images and infographics

The internet is still infographic-mad. You have probably seen a number of them doing the rounds. The danger is posting recycled content that people have seen a million times before. Pictures with quotes on and daft scenes of sunsets with rubbish slogans can get tiresome quickly.

If you're a thought-leader and you've actually come up with a good line you'd like to have attributed to you, try making it into a graphic. Stay away from being cheesy, the key is resonating with your connections.

Some ideas:

- Ask a graphic designer to make an infographic to display some data you have collected

- Overlay a quote or insight of your own on to a background of your company colour

- Create a picture collage of photos from an event you have run or attended, or of a new product line. Add text that describes the event or adds price information

With every graphic and infographic, make sure it's visually appealing, is easy to read and understand, and adds value.

Pro tip: credit any source you use for images.

How often: Monthly if possible
Ease/time: 2
Effect: 4

Idea 30: Share your press coverage

LinkedIn is the best platform on which to share your PR successes. Whilst the Facebook likes you'll achieve for a similar post is a great ego boost, it's unlikely to generate any leads.

LinkedIn, however, especially if you're a B2B company or a B2C company looking for collaborators, is perfect for getting on the radar of decision makers through great PR stories. There's always a chance that it will go viral if it's a particularly appealing achievement or cause (and a good picture never goes amiss).

This idea can be as simple as sharing a link to the coverage or just a picture of the coverage with an explanation of what happened.

Pro tip: adopt the right tone when sharing these types of story. Don't be too gushing or it will look like you're milking it; don't be too blasé or you'll come across arrogant (unless it's tongue in cheek blasé-ness). Be humble about it – be happy, grateful and at least a little bit excited.

How often: When you get great coverage
Ease/time: 4.5
Effect: 5

Idea 31: Showcase your work

Individuals and businesses alike should do this wherever possible. If you are a project-based business and these projects can be visually demonstrated, sharing them on LinkedIn is a humble way of showing off.

Again, don't overdo it. Think quality over quantity.

This can be a very effective way of showcasing both your work and the type of clients you work with. Half the issue people have with referrals is they get introductions to the wrong type or size of business. This exercise helps educate your network.

Examples:

- Pictures of equipment you have installed or purchased

- Your own products on display

- Before and after pictures, a situation before your services and then after (we know an electrician who sees awful fuse/wire boxes and then transforms them into neat and safe places that comply with the necessary regulations)

- Products and services of your client, or awards they've won

- A story about a client of yours and how you helped them

- An article you have featured in, a news story that mentions you, your company or a team member

How often: Every few weeks
Ease/time: 3
Effect: 5

Idea 32: Ask for opinions from your audience

Some of the most popular content on LinkedIn comes from individuals asking their connections which design they prefer for their new book cover, packaging design, or logo concept.

People love being asked their opinion.

It gives them a sense of value and importance having been able to help a fellow professional, even if they don't know you. Upon seeing your ideas, everyone will get an idea of which one they like. Everyone thinks they know what a good design is and which will sell best. Even people who don't know you may comment with their preference.

Simply ask which of the three designs is their favourite – a,b or c. Don't forget to use your final decision as an excuse to get back in touch with voters, to tell them why you went with (or didn't go with!) their choice.

It's the perfect way to generate some awareness and build up of a new book, product or brand launch with the potential to reach thousands of new people. We did it with the book cover of #*Winning at Social Media*!

How often: When the opportunity arises
Ease/time: 3
Effect: 5

Idea 33: LinkedIn isn't Facebook

Avoid commenting on stupid competitions or algebra problems or those "comment with the word you saw first?"-type posts.

Have some self-respect.

Every time you feel like getting involved, remember that this activity could be shown to any number of your professional network. Get a grip.

What does it say to your network that you a) idly scroll LinkedIn b) have the time to comment on this rubbish c) think that other people care that you saw 'success' first on a grid of 200 letters or that you worked out a banana + a pineapple + a coconut = 11. It's primary school algebra.

The only people that win here are the people and businesses that post this utter garbage, and even they look silly.

How often: Never

Idea 34: Write longer pieces in a post

If you have more to say than will fit into an update, or perhaps you want something to hang around for longer than a few hours, write a longer piece by publishing a post. Posts will also sit prominently on your profile.

To begin, simply click on the "publish a post" option towards the top of your home screen.

LinkedIn posts are akin to blog posts but they'll show up on your connections' feeds as a notification when they're published. These posts serve a number of purposes. First, ensuring you stay in people's minds, second, portraying yourself as a thought-leader and an expert in your field and, third, generating more traffic to your site.

These posts provide a medium through which to be more opinionated than you might be on your company's site and they can be much shorter than a commercial blog – only 300-400 words rather than 800-2000.

Successful posts not only need to read well but they must be interesting and relevant to your audience for greater reach and engagement.

A bonus is the ability to generate web traffic by linking some of your site's content within the text of the post. Only do this when appropriate; don't write artificially to create a link opportunity and stick to one or two links per post. Whilst this won't contribute directly to your search-engine optimisation (SEO), you will generate some clicks to your site.

Pro tip: once you start doing this, it can be tempting to publish posts all the time. Eventually, people become numb to these updates, especially if your posts aren't particularly interesting. Stick to a great piece every couple of weeks if you have time. As per usual; quality > quantity.

How often: Monthly
Ease/time: 1.5
Effect: 2.5 – 5 depending on how good they are!

Idea 35: Share "today's office"

If you do a lot of work on the road or around the country and even the globe, posting a picture of what your office looks like on any given day can make for interesting content. This isn't just about posting a picture of you at a beach bar with a cocktail in front of you – that's just annoying – but a view from a different coffee shop, cityscape and the odd abroad shot adds value to your audience.

It also creates the impression that you're busy, work out and about and that you're maybe not doing too badly for yourself. Humans are drawn to successful and busy people. In some industries, giving this impression is very valuable.

How often: Monthly
Ease/time: 3
Effect: 3

Idea 36: Make your company profile exceptional

There's no getting around this one. A great company profile underpins so much of your page's success and it's simply down to you putting in the effort.

Optimise your company profile by ensuring all the information asked for is completed, your company logo is actually used as the main 'square logo' picture and you have a suitable banner image.

It's now important to provide an effective description of your company. Convey your ethos and be clear about exactly what your company does and whom it helps. Make sure there are some key words included so people have a better chance of finding you when searching for companies like yours. Along these lines, make sure your company specialities are listed accurately and don't list too many. You can't *specialise* in 20 different fields – I don't care who you are.

- Your profile description can be up to 2000 characters (around 200 of which show before you have to click 'see more')

- **Banner image** - Minimum 646x220 pixels, PNG/JPEG/GIF format, Maximum 2 MB, landscape layout, image should be wider rather than taller.

- **Add a square logo** - Minimum 300 x 300 pixels, 400 x 400 pixels is the recommended size PNG/JPEG/GIF format, Maximum 4 MB, square layout.

You can also add featured, showcase pages for certain products or services that you offer that may be targeted at a specific audience. LinkedIn doesn't offer a draft option for these so ensure they are created and approved in a word document before uploading.

From LinkedIn's own site: "showcase pages are designed for spotlighting a brand, business unit, or initiative. Create a page for aspects of your business with their own messages and audience segments to share with." For example, it makes sense that Microsoft has separate pages for Excel, PowerPoint and Word.

IMPORTANT: even if you haven't yet set up a LinkedIn company page, LinkedIn may have set one up automatically. This means a) you need to claim ownership of it and b) if you're reluctant to set one up and optimise it – there might be a pretty average-looking one sitting there already for anyone to find and tut at.

How often: ASAP
Ease/time: 2.5
Effect: 5

Idea 37: Ensure your employees have updated LinkedIn profiles

LinkedIn shows how many employees your company has on LinkedIn and who they are. If you have employees who do not list your company as their employer, you're missing out on exposure.

Make sure they say something useful about your company in their summary as well as in their 'experience' section. Again, this is all useful signposting and advertising to your extended network that your business should benefit from.

On the other hand, ensure that any previous employees have clearly marked when their employment at your company ended and double-check that the role and information they provided about their work at your company is correct. Ensure they have not mentioned any client names or other information you deem private.

Some people argue that giving away the names of their employees on LinkedIn makes them easier to poach. However, if an up-to-date LinkedIn profile is all that's standing between an existing employee and their future employer you have more deep-rooted HR issues to deal with.

Pro tip: create a standard company description and ensure that current and future employees include it in their 'experience' section. This helps to give the company a uniform presence.

How often: ASAP
Ease/time: 2
Effect: 3

Idea 38: Post regular updates to your company page

LinkedIn suggests that posting 20 times per month will ensure 60% of your page followers will see at least one update. That's pretty much one update every single working day of the month to reach just 60% of the people who *already* follow your company.

Whilst this might seem excessive, finding something interesting to talk about and sharing it at various times during the week will increase brand exposure and ensure you stay in the minds of your network. If you genuinely add value to your audience, the frequency of posts shouldn't be an issue and, besides, most of them will only see a few posts each.

Pro tip: use a scheduling tool like Buffer or Hootsuite to schedule timeless content in advance.

How often: Up to daily
Ease/time: 2.5
Effect: 4

Idea 39: Encourage team members to engage with company posts

LinkedIn's current algorithm is very simple: your posts and the actions people make on that post show up on people's timelines. This means when your team members like or share a company post, some of their connections will know about it.

This is a simple way to significantly increase the reach of company page content and the clicks through to the page, whilst ensuring your company has a united presence across its team members.

Pro tip: when you have written an update from your company page, copy the link and send it to your team via email. Ask them to open the link and click 'like' and let them know it only takes a second!

How often: Weekly
Ease/time: 3
Effect: 4

Idea 40: Share company blogs on your company page

Drive more web traffic to your key content using LinkedIn. Simply share the URL of the blog you want people to read and add some tempting text. Use either intriguing language or tell people exactly what they're going to get from reading it – they create a similar effect.

E.g.

The three biggest mistakes I see marketers make every day and what I recommend doing instead: [LINK]

…and

Find out how to increase your web traffic using LinkedIn [LINK]

These types of post form the content you should be sharing multiple times per week. You can share the same blog more than once but use different text and try posting it at a different time of the day and working week.

Pro tip: pull out your favourite tip from the article and explain it within the LinkedIn post itself, inviting the reader to click the link to see more.

How often: Weekly
Ease/time: 3
Effect: 3

Idea 41: Try sponsored updates or advertisements

LinkedIn's paid-for sponsorship of company page posts is akin to promoting a Facebook post to a targeted audience. Stick to engaging, interesting posts with a clear call to action and a great image.

Decide whether you want maximum exposure, maximum clicks or if you want to generate sales and leads to your website. The type of post and calls to actions vary wildly for these and there's an element of trial and error here...

To start this process go to 'business services > advertise > manage ads, create campaign'. You can then create a 'sponsored updates' campaign. After choosing the company page you wish to send sponsored updates from, you have the opportunity to create your audience.

Your audience can be specified according to the following:

- Location
- Company name
- Company industry
- Company size
- Job title, job function, job seniority
- Fields of study, degrees, schools, skills, groups
- Gender and age

As you select characteristics of your audience, on the right-hand side of the page LinkedIn will tell you how many people fulfil this criteria.

You can then choose the updates you'd like to show to this audience, select your budget and begin.

Use the company page analytics that LinkedIn provides to judge the return achieved from sponsoring the post. This will help you tailor your next post and determine how much you want to spend on future efforts.

Pro tip: use Google analytics to measure the number of people sent to your website from LinkedIn, before and after your sponsor company updates.

How often: Monthly or more if they work well for your business
Ease/time: 2
Effect: 2-4 (there's only one way to find out…)

Idea 42: Post your vacancies on LinkedIn

Recruitment is a costly exercise in terms of time, agency fees and the cost of hiring the wrong person. Furthermore, posting jobs with agencies can narrow your options to their roster and to people actively seeking roles. Roles posted to LinkedIn can be viewed by anyone and the platform is pretty good at advertising the role to the right people (including those not actively seeking new roles).

A well-written description with a clear start date, wage bracket and selection criteria will attract dozens of applicants, all of whom you can assess quickly using their profile. At the time of writing, LinkedIn refunds your listing fee if you don't receive at least ten applicants.

It's incredibly low-cost compared with a recruitment agency and it's another way of generating brand awareness. Even if you don't end up hiring someone through LinkedIn, you'll have plenty of CVs to look at to help you assess the talent out there and choose the right person.

This is one of LinkedIn's biggest revenue generators but relatively few companies actually use it.

How often: As necessary
Ease/time: 2
Effect: 3-5

Idea 43: Try company posts to "targeted audiences"

Note: this will only work if you have a large amount of followers on your company LinkedIn page.

Note: this is not paid-for advertising.

This is similar to defining an audience on Facebook, but with professionals who follow your company. You can target individuals who follow your company by their company size, location, function, seniority and industry but, currently, there must be at least 100 people remaining in your search results. If you're lucky enough to have tens of thousands of followers, you can be fairly specific with who sees your post.

This function is perhaps better used to discount certain people, rather than target them. For example, if you have followers around the globe but you're promoting something to the UK market, post to people in the UK. If you're posting a job description, you can exclude employees.

Worth knowing about.

How often: When you send a specific type of update
Ease/time: 3
Effect: 2-3 depending on follower numbers.

Idea 44: Build your email database

LinkedIn is a great place to pick up new subscribers to your mailing list. Offer something of value to your audience; an eBook, a checklist, a password-protected video etc. and tell them all they need to do is sign up for it. This is a great tactic to use on both your personal and business profiles.

Ideally, people receive an automated response with the promised nugget of information as soon as they sign up – JC Social Media gives away a free LinkedIn cheat sheet!

People love free stuff that is of value to them, even if they have to part with an email address to obtain it. These LinkedIn posts, clearly stating that they're giving away certain information, guides or downloads tend to do very well from an engagement perspective.

Pro tip: add value. Give information away for free and charge for implementation.

How often: Monthly
Ease/time: 4
Effect: 4

Idea 45: Use LinkedIn analytics on the company page

The data contained within your company LinkedIn analytics isn't super detailed but it tells you a lot about the content you share. The most valuable information is how many engagements each piece of content generates and what the trends are.

Look at your most successful posts: when were they shared, what was the call to action, what was the image used, what did the post promise? Now look at unsuccessful posts – the ones with no (or very few) comments, likes, shares or clicks – how do they compare?

Use this information to improve your content distribution and maximise engagements with each posts. The goal is continuous improvement.

How often: Analyse monthly
Ease/time: 4
Effect: 4

Idea 46: Create and run your own LinkedIn group

This is a key tactic for thought-leaders and can be both an arena in which to generate leads and something you can turn into a business, itself.

Being the owner of a LinkedIn group puts you at the forefront of a sector and rapidly increases your visibility amongst members. You can also govern what happens and what is said in the group.

Groups of more than a few thousands members all within a specific industry or role are inherently valuable and many have successfully moved to successful (paid!) membership organisations.

Before you create one, thoroughly search LinkedIn for similar groups. Try a few different combinations of words and phrases that might describe groups you could start. If similar ones exist – how well developed are they? What could you do to improve on their model and be more successful?

If there are already well-established groups within your sector, could you create a smaller niche group for just some of the members? If there aren't any well-established groups within your sector, ensure there is a need for one before going ahead and starting one. Perhaps speak in person to a few potential members and get their opinion.

How often: As soon as you have the resources and ideas, as it requires weekly action
Ease/time: 1
Effect: up to 5

Idea 47: Tag other people in updates asking for information

Some professionals use LinkedIn to source talent or professionals in certain sectors or with certain expertise. I.e. "can anyone recommend a graphic designer in Edgbaston?" Or "Can someone translate my script into Mandarin?"

Know someone who fits the bill? Know a graphic designer in Edgbaston or a translation specialist? Tag them in the comments section, which will send them a notification. Add a few personalised words as opposed to just writing their name, make it clear who makes the next move. Write something like "Jodie Cook is the person to speak with" or "I have worked with Jodie Cook and highly recommend her" or "Could you help, Jodie Cook?" Make sure you tag them properly in your response.

They'll thank you for it, even if it's not suitable for them. It shows you're looking out for others and that you're well connected. Hopefully they'll get the gig!

If someone does this for you, make sure you comment with your contact details as soon as possible. Be friendly and approachable – don't be a vulture! This is a great way to nurture leads.

Pro tip: seen a LinkedIn post asking for someone whose description you fit? Ask a friend to comment first to recommend you and then follow up with your contact details.

How often: Whenever possible
Ease/time: 4
Effect: 4

Idea 48: Export your LinkedIn contacts' email addresses

LinkedIn gives you the ability to export all of your contacts' details, including their email addresses. Some of your contacts will be more responsive to email communications so this is the perfect way of accruing them. If you or your business distributes great e-newsletters that generate good open and click rates as well as generating leads, this idea has great benefits.

Click 'my network > connections > settings (cog icon) > export LinkedIn connections'.

Pro tip: remember that email marketing is required to be 'opt-in', so make the necessary arrangements to ensure you are not spamming! By law you also must include an unsubscribe option on any emailing you do.

How often: Quarterly to keep updated (but after idea 2)
Ease/time: 5
Effect: 3.5

Idea 49: Add to your email signature and website

Make it easy for people to find and connect with you by adding your (now personalised) LinkedIn URL to your email signature, business cards, and contact page on your website.

To attract people who have hit your website, you can add a LinkedIn button in the side bar or footer. Create the button from:

https://www.linkedin.com/public-profile/settings

And clicking 'create a badge' in the bottom right of the page.

Ask a web developer if you require help in adding the code to your site.

You could add your personal profile to a personal site or create a follow button for your company's LinkedIn page from a company site. The more followers your company page has, the more reach and influence it has.

How often: Once
Ease/time: 3
Effect: 3

Idea 50: See what your classmates are up to

Find your university's page on LinkedIn – either by a quick search or clicking through from your education section.

Select 'Alumni' from the left hand menu.

Alumni have a strange but powerful bond with each other. It's amazing just how powerful it is. Even though tens of thousands of people have attended your university, there's an evident loyalty between them and this is a great way to start a conversation with people in an organisation you'd like to talk to.

This area might also be a good place to find people you should already be connected with, just as discussed way back in idea 2. This should act as a bank of new connections and discussions.

How often: Every few months
Ease/time: 4
Effect: 3

Final words

So there you have it. 50 great ideas for LinkedIn that will help you take your offline and online networking a step further, to generate better business relationships and win clients. We hope you've enjoyed the ideas and that you put some of them in to action **right now.** We'd love to know your thoughts on the book and if it's helped you, we'd be really grateful for a review on Amazon.

Remember we've put together a handy checklist in printable format available from www.jcsocialmedia.com/great-ideas.

Look out for the other titles in the 50 Great Ideas series including Twitter, Facebook and easy SEO. Jodie Cook also penned **#Winning at Social Media, it's all about the interaction**. #Winning is an in-depth look at social media theory and prescriptive tactics to use on Twitter and LinkedIn to find and engage with members of your target audience.

You'll find more great tips and ideas for social media on the JC Social Media blog.

Thanks for reading.

Jodie and Ben.

Printed by Amazon Italia Logistica S.r.l.
Torrazza Piemonte (TO), Italy

ANGRY SINS

A DOC HUNTER NOVEL

By

C. E. Nelson